Scrappy Flock of Sheep

David Libby

First Published in 2021 by David Libby

Cover Design by Derek Beaudoin

978-1-68474-293-6
Imprint: Lulu.com

**To Everyone who Does Crazy Work in the Name of
Jesus and Makes Enemies Because of it**

You Are My Heroes

CONTENTS

INTRODUCTION

There are certain times in life where a choice seems so obvious that you can't imagine not making it. This was one of those.

In early 2019, our church decided to lease a part of our land, which would be used for a Village of tiny homes for houseless[1] people in our community. The project would be funded through the Joint Office of Homeless Services in Multnomah County, while local nonprofit Do Good Multnomah would run the program and connect residents with services and housing.

There are thousands of people in Portland without homes, without safety nets, and without a support network of any kind. Housing prices are astronomical here. Single-person studio apartments rent for $1500/mo., while thousands of folks sleep in the cold. It's wrong that people are, and will forever be, unable to have a place to live. It's unjust that people have to live with the crippling mental illness that comes from living on the street.

Suddenly, we were presented with an opportunity to provide this land, and the program and security will be run by a nonprofit with a good track record, and for whom a few of my good and trusted friends work. Our part of the project was simply to offer the land. If we allowed others to use the land that was currently sitting

---

[1] Many who live in housing instability now prefer the term *houseless* to *homeless*. The term "home" can refer to community and social connection among other things. What a houseless person is missing is a *house*. Therefore, I will typically use the term "houseless" instead of "homeless" throughout this book. For a longer explanation of the reasoning for using the term *houseless*, see "Why Do We Say Houseless?" Do Good Multnomah, June 15, 2019, https://dogoodmultnomah.org/blog/why-do-we-say-houseless

dormant, people could move from homelessness to housed and safe with a new lease on life.

This was a no brainer.

Doing something about homelessness in Portland would require us to offer some of our land.
That's it.
That's all.
We made a pitch to the church, our church members voted, and the project was publicly announced.

The reaction from the community was intense.
Explosive.
Nuclear might be a better word.
We had no idea what we signed up for, or how aggressive the reaction would be.
We had no clue of the battles we would fight to make this Village a reality.

This is the story of a project.
More than that, it is the story of a naive group of ordinary Christians struggling to bring light and goodness into the lives of some of Portland's most vulnerable population.
We failed often.
Sometimes it was difficult to figure out the right or wrong way to do something.

The thing about failing is that you learn a lot.

This is the story of a project.

6

This is the story of a success, and tons of failure.
This is the story of a compassionate church, who was
often bad at compassion.

PART I: PLANNING

You want to close your eyes
You want to make believe this tangled web you weave
Is nowhere near the place you sleep
While other people's lives are cheap
And all of this is someone else's problem
-Five Iron Frenzy, "Someone Else's Problem"

In early 2019, my friend Andy approached me with an idea about using my church's property to build temporary homes for houseless folks in Portland. This was not the first time that I had considered using our property for housing. When I arrived at our church in 2015, I was immediately struck with how large our property was, and how little of it was used on a regular basis.

Our church is over a hundred years old, and has been through a few iterations. Over the last century-plus, a small building became a large building. A second wing was built onto our building. We acquired a large field across the street, as well as two separate parking lots.

Our little church owns a lot of property.

It occurred to me one week while writing a devotion for our church's offering time, that we regularly ask our congregation to practice good stewardship of their money and resources. Meanwhile, we own one enormous church building, another three-story building with dozens of classrooms, two parking lots, and an enormous field. We run one church service per week, a handful of small group gatherings, and we loan out our space to various community events. We don't hold close to enough gatherings during the week to warrant the amount of space that we own.

I realized that we own what is easily one of the largest properties in our neighborhood, and we were not using it as best we could.

I dreamed about what could be done with our property. We discussed the possibility of turning our third floor into a preschool, but quickly learned how much money it would cost to remodel the building for that purpose. Plus, at the time we did not have any leads on a preschool that was needing space, and we had nobody in our congregation who wanted to lead a preschool.

We discussed turning the field into a community park. This idea actually went pretty far. We discussed play equipment, benches, and tables to beautify the community. However, we also considered the potential downsides. The field would be considerably harder to mow with benches and play equipment constantly in use. Our insurance would be much higher due to the potential of children getting injured on the property. Most concerning, however, was the thought that a kid might step on a dirty needle. Houseless folks regularly sleep in this grassy field. We do periodic sweeps of the field where we find needles and broken glass. Kids often walk through this field, and many more would do so if a playground was present. Plus, there is already a large community park three blocks from the church. We found it redundant to build another, considering the risks involved, and the proximity of another park.

The most compelling idea to me, however, was housing. We have a second parking lot that we never use for anything, ever. We also have a large field that functions as a glorified dog park most days. There is a ton of space that could potentially be used for affordable housing. When I showed up at St. Johns Christian Church in 2015, I had no interest in housing justice. Housing would not have been in the top 100 issues in which I was concerned. Sure, I was aware that homelessness was an issue especially in Portland. However, my concern for houseless folks only stretched to offering them food and clothing. Housing as a justice issue was nowhere near the top of my list.

It didn't take long for it to become my main focus.

Behind our church is an alleyway in which houseless people often sleep. There is an overhang in the alley which people use to stay dry during rainy nights.

Here in Portland, every night is a rainy night.

Many mornings, I have to go outside and ask people to gather their stuff and leave. It's the hardest part of my job, by far. The compassionate side of me knows that people are simply looking for a safe, dry place to sleep. On the other hand, there are times when fights have broken out in this alleyway, and we occasionally find needles as well. Someone once detonated a pipe bomb in our dumpster. Since kids regularly walk through the alley, I have to make sure that houseless folks do not remain in the alley long-term.

One morning, I was preparing for our weekly staff meeting, when I saw somebody who had slept the previous night in the alley. Our meeting was in ten minutes, so I rushed outside to quickly tell this guy that he had to leave. I tried talking with him, but he didn't respond. He was completely focused on trying to pull a tire off of his bike wheel. I nudged him with my foot, and said, "Hey, dude, I need you to leave."
He responded, "Alright, fine. I'm about to throw myself off of the bridge anyway."

That stopped me in my tracks.

I sat down next to him and asked what was going on. He talked about a friend leaving town, and his mom's bad health, and how he had nowhere to go. He said that he was moving from place to place, because there were certain people who didn't like him, and wanted to hurt him. "And now," he said, "I can't get this tube on my damn bike tire. It's not working, so I'm going to throw myself off of the bridge."

I texted our staff and told them that I'd be late to the meeting.

I sat with this guy for over an hour and listened to him talk about his struggles over the previous few years.

He wasn't a drug addict, but occasionally used when things were too overwhelming. His family life was, in a word, terrible. He had no friends and no connection to any services.

I helped him put the bike tire on (it took forever....I'm not the most handy person), and eventually he was on his way.

Another morning, there was a girl sleeping on the doorstep of the church when I arrived. She was disheveled and exhausted. I grabbed her some coffee from inside the building and sat down to chat with her. She had recently left an abusive relationship and didn't have family or a support network in Portland. Like the gentleman in the previous story, this girl had considered suicide a number of times. As luck would have it, we had just finished our annual garage sale at the church and had some unsold clothing that we had not yet donated to a thrift store. She rummaged through the clothes for a couple of hours, and I listened to her talk about her life and struggles.

I think about these folks a lot. There are people in this world who are often seen as a "nuisance." There are people who are loud, unkempt, and who occasionally cause problems. I often forget that behind the "nuisance" is typically a lot of trauma. The guy in the alley reminded me of that, as did the girl on our doorstep, and countless other houseless people over the years. Over time, homelessness has shifted for me from *abstract concept* to *absolute crisis*, affecting and impacting people that I know and love.

Discrimination toward houseless people can be some of the worst kinds of prejudice. A study in Psychological Science argued that groups stereotyped as hostile and incompetent, which includes houseless people and addicts, suffer worse than simply a general prejudice; they suffer dehumanization.[2] So many prejudices exist in our world today, from racism, to homophobia, to transphobia, to sexism, to ageism; but the dehumanization experienced by houseless and addicts can be absolutely crippling.

When I think of this kind of dehumanization, I think of the story from Mark 5, where a man is chained up by the crowds because of his demon possession. He is in such a state that the masses have no idea what to do with him, so they chain him to some rocks.

I also think of the story Jesus tells in Luke 16. In this story, a wealthy man lived the life that most of us probably wish we had. Nice house, lots of money, lots of food. There's another man in the story named Lazarus, who is covered in sores and has no money, no food, and no home. When Jesus describes Lazarus as "having sores," you immediately know that this is a person that the general population would be disgusted to look at. I think of many of the houseless people I encounter daily in Portland. The kind of dehumanization that they experience is also the kind of thing I imagine Lazarus experiences on a daily basis.

---

[2] Harris, Lasana T., and Susan T. Fiske. "Dehumanizing the Lowest of the Low: Neuroimaging Responses to Extreme Out-Groups." Psychological Science 17, no. 10 (October 2006): 847–53. https://doi.org/10.1111/j.1467-9280.2006.01793.x

The rich man finds judgment and agony at the end of his life, while Lazarus finds peace and comfort next to Abraham after he dies. Abraham tells the no-longer-rich man that there is a great chasm between him and Lazarus. This chasm is not new, however. In their previous lives, there was a great chasm between the two as well. The rich man had much, and Lazarus had nothing. Lazarus wanted anything he could possibly receive, including the wasted food from the rich man's table. Picture a houseless person who was so hungry, he would be grateful to receive the last third of your second McDonald's hamburger that you were too full to finish and promptly threw in the garbage. There was a great chasm between the two, both in life and in death. The rich man knew nothing of the needs of Lazarus, as the rich man's needs were all taken care of. He was safe, and he remained in his safety.

When I read these stories about rich folks who don't give to or even acknowledge the houseless who are covered in sores, and those who chain up the demon possessed, I can't help but think about rich American Christians who are blind to the needs of the houseless man who is strung out on heroin and needs support. I'm forced to think about rich American Christians who deafen themselves to the needs of the veteran with PTSD who is unable to take care of him or herself.

Throughout scripture, God cares deeply about the poor, the vulnerable, and the oppressed. This story makes that truth crystal clear. Responding to the needs of others by thinking primarily of oneself is not the way of

Christ; it is the way that leads to torment. Over the years, my heart's desire has become to try and bridge the chasm between rich and poor; wealthy and houseless; healthy and covered in sores.

By the time Andy approached me in 2019 about starting a village to help houseless people, I had already spent years trying to find a solution to the housing crisis in our city. I had already considered how our church might be able to use our land to provide a roof and walls to the most disenfranchised among us.

I had no idea what this would look like, or how it would operate, but I was ready. Our church was ready. It was time for us to steward our land well.

Our church voted 94% in favor of leasing our land for the Village.
The hard work was over.
The Village was a success, and everybody in the neighborhood and city was happy during every step of the process.

THE END

Nah, actually a ton of people were pissed.

We formulated what we felt was a solid plan for rolling out the news about our project. Monday morning following the vote tabulation, members of Do Good Multnomah and the Joint Office of Homeless Services walked door to door handing out informational flyers showing our detailed plans for the Village. We made sure to clarify that none of the plans were finalized. We made clear to everyone who asked that there would be informational meetings, a good neighbor agreement, and community involvement in the whole process.
For the most part, those clarifiers fell on deaf ears.

Every day, our church received dozens of phone calls with questions about the project. We answered to the best of our ability, but much of the project was still theoretical at this point. We did not yet have a firm timeline, an architect, a developer, or a contractor. We had mountains of red tape to cut through in order to make the Village a reality; from zoning laws to parking issues.

I heard whispers of multiple neighborhood groups that were gathering in opposition to the project. The organizer of one of these groups invited me over for lunch, where I learned of the dozens of grievances from the neighborhood. Many of the early concerns, surprisingly, were not about the project itself. Rather, many neighbors felt betrayed and blindsided by the project, and felt that our church had kept them in the dark for months.

My co-pastor Janel and I spent the next month meeting one-on-one with many neighbors and community members, trying to answer as many questions as possible. Looking back, I now realize that regardless of how we unveiled this project, people would have been angry. However, at the time, we honestly felt the weight of our neighbors' feelings of hurt and betrayal. In no way did any of us at the church want to hurt our neighbors. However, we also knew that our neighborhood was not solely made up of homeowners. Many of our neighbors were suffering, freezing, and hungry. We wanted to provide a home for them.

A slew of local and statewide news stories aired shortly after the announcement of the Village project. These early news reports about our project were extremely positive. One local anchor exclaimed, "What a great way for a church to walk the talk." We were encouraged by the early buzz, and thought that it might drown out some of the naysayers.

However, after our worship service on Easter Sunday 2019, some of us noticed a small group of people in the field at our church, and a lady filming with an enormous camera. We could tell that something was happening for TV, but we were not sure what it was. I considered talking to the group, but also knew that if this were a negative news story, I could be ambushed with unexpected questions in front of the news cameras.

Sure enough, one of the anti-Village neighborhood groups had contacted the news and asked for a story. That evening, a spotlight on our church aired on TV. This segment ended with a plea from a neighbor:

Come to the upcoming community informational meeting and vent your frustrations to the church.

And come, they did.

No one ever had much nice to say
I think they never liked you anyway
-My Chemical Romance, "Dead"

In early 2017, my body began to shut down. It began when I had a rough conversation with someone at our church. The conversation started poorly and ended in a walkout. From the moment my friend left the room, and for the following hour and a half, I was frozen. I could not move my body. I realized that since my friend left, I had stared at the same spot on the table. My hands were both flat on the table, and my legs were both planted firmly on the floor. For ninety minutes, I attempted to will my body to move. I tried telling my index finger to budge. My head continued staring at the table, and all of my limbs were completely frozen. My mind was working, but my body remained immobile. It was a complete bodily shutdown, and it seemingly came out of nowhere. Never before had I been unable to move. Never before had I lost command over my limbs. It was 90 minutes before I was able to lift my index finger, then my other fingers, and finally my arms, legs, and head.

Throughout the following year, bodily shutdowns exactly like this one continued. Often when I would have a conversation with someone that became heated, I would find myself unable to move from anywhere between 20 and 90 minutes. Each time, I would attempt to force my legs, arms, head, or even fingers and toes to move, and each time, I would be incapable. This phenomenon became worse over time. I noticed myself powerless to move even when I did not have a rough conversation with another person. If I merely thought about someone who caused me stress, my body could shut down. If I looked at my schedule for the day and realized had too many tasks to accomplish in the time allotted, my body often shut down. It started affecting my work, my home life, and even my general emotional state. I frequently started hyperventilating, seemingly for no reason. I could no longer sleep through the night. After a year of this, I made an appointment with a therapist, who ultimately diagnosed me with anxiety and depression.

For a long time, we tried to avoid medication; to treat my mental illness solely through practices like grounding techniques, meditation practices, and journaling. These were helpful for quite a while, and I was able to avoid pursuing medication until That Meeting.

Shortly after announcing our plan to lease our property for the Village, we announced a community meeting to explain our vision and to be available for Q & A. We expected a small but passionate group of people to show up at the church. I had already been informed that there were people discussing the possibility of a lawsuit against our church, and one neighbor had already put his house on the market because he did not want to live next to a homeless Village. People were angry, and I knew it. However, I also believed that once the community took the time to hear about our project in detail, they would come around and support what we were doing. I believed that our team could deal well with this small group of neighbors.

Except it was not a small group of neighbors.

Five hundred people showed up to our meeting, and many of them were *so mad. So, so mad.*

Our plans for the meeting quickly derailed, and it became a 2+ hour screamfest. Some highlights include:

1. One dude calling all houseless people "parasites."
2. A younger girl explaining to the hostile crowd how gentrification is at the root of many of the problems in St. Johns (her speech was met with cries of "Who are you to tell me where I'm allowed to buy a house?").
3. Our church being repeatedly accused of 'using' houseless people to make a quick buck.
4. Some dude creeping closer and closer behind our administrative pastor (her husband was ready to thump the dude).
5. The crowd mocking and laughing at one of the leaders of the project because of how emotionally invested he was in the project.

It was a cool meeting. Very fun. 10/10 would recommend.

The meeting ended, and after I got my bearings and went back to my office to recover, my body shut down again. For an hour and a half, I stared at my feet, unable to move; unable to think; unable to imagine a way to move forward. I got home and checked my phone. Dozens of strangers had emailed and messaged me, telling me how poorly I had handled the meeting, and sharing their disappointment in our church and my leadership. I read until I couldn't read anymore, then I chased some sleeping pills with a glass of wine and went to bed.

For the following two days, I was unable to get out of bed for anything other than to grab some water or go to the bathroom. I lay on the bed with the covers pulled completely over my head, like a five-year-old protecting himself from monsters. I could not face the outside world, the neighbors, society, my wife, or my kids. I felt like a failure, and believed the entire town hated me. That whole week, I saw myself as the most hated person in the neighborhood of St. Johns. My phone lit up with email and Facebook notifications from people who were furious with me. I read a few, and turned my phone back off, pulling the covers back over my head.

For two days, I stayed in my bedroom.
For two days, I remained under the covers.
For two days I hid from the world.

At the time I was training for a half marathon, but I couldn't get myself to go for a run. Leaving the house meant facing the neighbors, and I simply could not do that.

Over the next few days and weeks, the bodily shutdowns became more frequent. The panic attacks became worse. And every moment I was overwhelmed with the belief that the rest of the neighborhood hated my guts. All the while, I carried the shame of wondering why this impacted me so greatly. After all, I wasn't assaulted. People weren't camped outside of my home. I hadn't been doxxed. I had my job. I had my family. I had friends that loved me.

Honestly, all that occurred was a couple hours of screaming. It really wasn't that bad. So why did it impact me like it had? Politicians, sports figures, musicians, and actors deal with this stuff on a daily basis, and I crumbled after one single incident. I felt weak; powerless. I wished I had never gone forward with the project. I wished that I had never become pastor of this church. I wished that I had never gone into ministry at all. I didn't feel strong enough for this line of work. I wanted to hang it all up. I wanted to cancel the project and quit my job.

In my lowest moments, I wanted to die.

I'd had suicidal thoughts before, but they were becoming more common.

And stronger.

Darker.

When I had the strength to do so, I called my therapist and asked if she had an emergency opening. My thoughts were spiraling, and I was afraid where it would ultimately lead. Over the next couple of days, I had a frank discussion with my therapist and my doctor about medication. Later that week I started taking Lexapro.

Having taken medication for a couple of years, I can attest that it has greatly helped reduce my anxiety and depression. I'm still depressed and anxious much of the time, and I still have panic and anxiety attacks, but they are much less frequent. Most importantly, the suicidal thoughts are few and far between. I cannot imagine making it to the end of this project without the help of medication.

When I first started telling people that I was in therapy for anxiety and depression, a friend from long ago contacted me and told me that they thought I had a demon. I understood where this person was coming from, as I also grew up with an understanding that mental illness was something demonic. While I grew past that belief over time, I still had an internalized understanding that having a mental illness was a sort of weakness. I felt as though I should be able to manage my anxiety and depression; to "just stop being sad."

However, I have come to realize that my own mental health problems are much more simply explained: my serotonin levels were unbalanced in some way. That's all.

That Meeting was a harsh trigger for me, and my brain was unable to help me through that time. Medication and therapy helped me cope with life in a way in which I was previously unable.

It pains me to think how many projects are abandoned by churches because of community resistance. It pains me to think how many pastors over the years have buckled under the weight of community pressure.

I wonder how many pastors suffer from mental health problems, and how many of these pastors are crippled by meetings like the one at our church?

Might therapy or medication have saved these projects?

Might they have even saved some lives?

My own battle with anxiety and depression is not over. It likely never will be. However, I am having considerably less thoughts of suicide, and that's a positive thing. We also successfully completed our Village project.

All of this thanks in large part to therapy and medication.

I hope that mental health problems will be more normalized in the future.

I hope pastors can be honest about their mental states, and seek help when needed.

I hope to see God do some incredible things through the Church because Christian leaders are mentally and emotionally healthy.

Before the vote was finalized, our elders, Do Good Multnomah, and the Joint Office of Homeless Services met together to make a communications rollout plan. One important piece of the rollout was to designate one of our church leaders to be the main point of communication for the neighborhood. While the church would not be in charge of the design, construction, financing, or programming, we were an important player in the planning and implementing of the village.

One of our elders, Bud, was quick to offer his services. Bud has always been one to jump at the opportunity to involve himself in the work of the church. He does not have an ego about the work that he does; he simply believes in the work of our church and wants to help it be successful. He has always demonstrated a servant's heart and attitude. With Bud's volunteerism, everyone was content with the plan. After the vote, we would go public, and Bud would respond to the few questions from the neighborhood.

The day that we distributed flyers announcing the village, Bud received over 50 calls, a considerable amount of which were forceful and heated. He called me a bit flustered, saying "People are asking a bunch of questions, and I have no idea what to tell them. I told them about our upcoming community meeting, and I don't know what else to say."

We all regrouped to discuss how to respond to these calls. Bud had received dozens more since that first day, and we received hundreds of emails and messages on top of those. I expected Bud to back out of the process. I would have, were I in his shoes. He alone was receiving the vast majority of the calls early on in the process. However, when we gathered together, he simply said, "I told all of the neighbors that nothing has been finalized, but we're moving forward."

About a month later, a group of neighbors met together with a lawyer and threatened legal action against our church. For years, we as a church leadership have discussed what would happen if a lawsuit was brought against us. As our financial situation has always been poor, we would presumably close our doors. Now, we were being faced with the very real prospect of being sued by the neighborhood.

Bud was approached by the lawyer and a couple of neighbors about meeting with our leadership team. We sat down with them on a Sunday evening and listened to all of their concerns. Although these concerns seemed to us to be based in fear instead of reality, we also knew that this fear-based thinking could easily result in a very real lawsuit. We listened to the lawyer and the neighbors for about an hour. Afterward, we all sat down to discuss and debrief.

We looked to Bud first, and he said simply, "We said that we would listen to them, and we did. But we prayed about this project. We asked God if it was right for our church. We asked the church to vote on this, and they did. We know this is what God wants for our church. Now we keep moving forward."

A lot of things have spooked me over the past year and a half. I was yelled at by a room of 500 people. I was threatened with a lawsuit. Things have been said about my motives, my abilities, and my faith that have shocked me. I have wanted to quit this project dozens of times. I started anti-anxiety medication because of increased panic attacks and suicidal thoughts. I have sat alone at home, wishing that I could turn back the clock to January 2019, so that I could tell Andy that there was absolutely no way that our church was going to house a tiny home Village.

Bud is honestly much of the reason that this project made it to completion. His simple way of framing our journey showed me that we were in this together, and that we could keep going. Every time that I wanted to abandon this project altogether; when the process seemed too daunting or deflating; Bud helped me to continue taking the next step forward with his simple refrain:

We keep moving forward.

PART II: FIGHTING

The second time that the news asked me for an on-camera interview, it was for an extended story on faith communities who are working on sheltering and housing projects for houseless people. I was interviewed for over an hour in our church building. For the majority of the interview, I said nothing that could likely be considered controversial. I was careful to avoid antagonizing the neighborhood, as by this point we had been threatened with legal action.

However, something happens near the end of a long interview -- you become more comfortable and less guarded.

The interviewer ended our conversation by asking me, "What would you say to those community members who claim that by helping a small group of people, you are causing harm to the thousands of people already in St. Johns?" Earlier in the interview, I probably would have responded with more compassion toward our neighbors. However, by this point, I was a little more direct. I responded, "I understand that people fear what will happen with the housing prices in this neighborhood, and I'm sympathetic to that fear. However, there are people in our community who have nowhere to sleep. They don't have a roof at all. I understand the argument that folks have made - the claim that we're hurting 200 people in order to save 20. But those 20 do not have a house at all. And if I'm being asked to care for 200 people who have a house or 20 people who don't, I'm going to care for the 20."

The news, to my surprise and delight at the time, didn't air that answer. However, as time has progressed, I wish they had. The original announcement of the Village project had a massive effect on the discourse in St. Johns. Much was made of how "our church is destroying the community." People were furious with us.

And I get it.

If we solely consider numbers, then we were absolutely destroying the community. Inconveniencing many for the sake of a few is bad politics.

However, our church was not playing politics, and this was not about numbers. Whenever the status quo is shaken, some people become angry. The status quo is about keeping the largest amount of people content. But when there are people whose lives are hurt by the status quo being left alone, then something needs to change.

Is the 20 more important than the 200? In some ways, no. The 20 and the 200 both bleed the same. The 20 and the 200 are both loved by God. The 20 and the 200 both have value, purpose, and a future. However, the lives of the 20 and the 200 are wildly unequal. The 20 are not afforded the safety, the social standing, the dignity, or the wealth of the 200. Not by a long shot.

Justice does not mean that the 20 is more important than the 200 in general. But justice does require that we consider the 20 more important than the 200 right now.

We prioritized the needs of a few houseless folks over the desires of the greater community because there was inequality.

The Good Shepherd leaves the 99 to save the 1.

The Good Shepherd cares for the 20 at the expense of the 200.

The Good Shepherd calls us to do the same.

I went to see ELO on a Saturday night. It was rad. Jeff Lynne's voice is still so, so, so good. The opener was Dhani Harrison.

Seriously, it was an incredible night.

The evening was, however, soured a little bit by a text I received near the start of the concert:

Just a warning, a group of neighbors is planning to protest outside of the church tomorrow morning before service.

Months prior, a group of people in Milwaukie (just outside of Portland) protested another church's program to help the homeless during their Sunday morning service. There were shouts, chants, signs raised in the air, and flyers handed out. News crews captured the whole event. It was pandemonium.[3]

I knew that this kind of event was probable at our church ever since I saw news clips of the Milwaukie protest. It was only a matter of time before signs, shouting, flyers, and news crews would come our way. For the remainder of the night I did my best to enjoy "Don't Bring Me Down," "Evil Woman," and "Mr. Blue Sky," trying not to dwell on the fact that the next morning was going to suuuuuuuuuuck.

---

[3] "Dozens of Neighbors Protest Overnight Homeless Shelter in Milwaukie Church Parking Lot," KGW News, May 5, 2019, https://www.kgw.com/article/news/local/homeless/dozens-of-neighbors-protest-overnight-homeless-shelter-in-milwaukie-church-parking-lot/283-f6491f29-d7ca-4949-bd36-ffb7ea12b44e

The next morning came, and so did the protesters. Dozens of folks from around the neighborhood handed out flyers and tried to convince anyone who would listen that our project was a terrible idea; one that would destroy our beautiful community. To be fair to these protesters, it was considerably more civil than the Milwaukie protest. Yes, there were flyers, and yes, there was heated opposition. However, there was no shouting, no signs, and best of all, no local media. The group aired their frustrations at myself and a few of our people, while most of our church members quickly raced into the building. The group stayed about fifteen minutes into our worship service's starting time, at which time the most vocal member of the group told the rest of the crowd that they should allow us to have our worship service.

A few of the protesters joined us for church that morning, which was lovely. This particular week, my sermon included a story about a time that I regretted not helping a houseless individual when I had the chance. When I wrote the sermon, I had no idea that protesters would be joining us for worship that Sunday. Sometimes things work out nicely (it's almost as if there was some sort of higher power who had something to speak into the hearts of those in our sanctuary that morning).

A member of our church stayed with the group of protesters as the rest of us gathered in the sanctuary for worship. The protesters huddled afterward to discuss their plans. He joined in to listen. The group planned to put a ton of pressure on our church for a while, and then let off for a bit, only to apply more pressure later. They would repeat this pattern until they exhausted us, hopefully causing us to abandon our plans for the Village.

And that's exactly what they did.

If there is one sentence that I would love never to hear again, it's "I'm not anti-homeless; I just think this is the wrong place." I have heard that sentence roughly 253,306,392 times in the past year. I heard it first from many individuals in the neighborhood, after we had announced our Village project. Anytime people came out against the project, they would offer this same refrain.

I assumed that "I'm not anti-homeless; I just think this is the wrong place" was unique to our area and situation. However, after we announced our project, other churches reached out and told me their stories of houseless advocacy. I began watching news stories of different housing and sheltering programs across the Northwest. In every single news story I read or watched, someone who lived near the program would say "I'm not anti-homeless; I just think this is the wrong place."

Every single time.

I totally understand this impulse. Nobody wants to be accused of being "anti-homeless." What kind of selfish monster wants to be thought of as prejudiced against homeless people? Defending oneself against the accusation of prejudice is totally reasonable.

So many thoughts swirl in my mind when I think about this sentence. First of all, it strikes me that "I'm not anti-homeless; I just think this is the wrong place" sounds eerily familiar to "I'm not racist; many of my friends are black," or "I'm not homophobic; I have a gay friend." We are so quick to defend ourselves against any kind of negative accusation. Again, this is totally understandable. Personally, I have a hard time acknowledging my own inherent racism and my prejudices. I especially don't like to admit that it's hard for me to look at a houseless person without being a bit disgusted. However, I understand that my own prejudices *are realities*, and things on which I need to continue to work. While I may be put off by people saying something like "I'm not racist; I have black friends" or "I'm not anti-homeless; I just think this is the wrong place," I need to first remind myself that I, too, have inherent prejudices that are problematic.

It occurs to me that "I'm not anti-homeless; I just think this is the wrong place" invites a number of follow-up questions:

- Who exactly considers this to be the wrong place?
- What makes this the wrong place? Who is hurt if this work is done in this place?
- Where would be the "right" place? Why would this new place be superior?
- If this kind of service to the homeless is wrong in *this* place, what other kind of service to the homeless *would* be acceptable in this place?

I don't have short, pithy, direct answers to many of these questions. Rather, I have a myriad of thoughts, reflections, and stories to share.

Did we take the time to really discover
How little we know about each other?
-Less Than Jake, "All My Best Friends are Metalheads"

There is an acronym that I had never heard before 2019: NIMBY. It stands for Not In My Back Yard. People opposed to many kinds of service work, specifically work focused on the homeless, are often referred to as NIMBYs. It is easy to understand why this nickname became used. When direct neighbors of sheltering programs consistently battle against the program and say things like "I'm not anti-homeless; I just think this is the wrong place," it becomes easy to stereotype all of these neighbors in a similar way.

I am uncomfortable anytime someone uses the NIMBY nickname, for the same reason that I become uncomfortable whenever Donald Trump uses demeaning nicknames for his political rivals: nicknames are used to demean and dehumanize. Rarely is a nickname given out of love or respect. Rather, nicknames are meant to caricature a person. They are used to make someone less comfortable with their appearance, intelligence, or character. They are used to stereotype people in unflattering ways.

I had an extremely high metabolism as a kid and was incredibly thin growing up. The things that people said about me in school caused me to have a very low opinion of my physical appearance. Still, to this day, I'm disgusted by the way that my body looks. A small nickname can have large consequences. Nicknames can be devastating and deadly.

James says that "the tongue is a small member, yet it boasts of great exploits. How great a forest is set ablaze by a small fire! And the tongue is a fire. The tongue is placed among our members as a world of iniquity; it stains the whole body, sets on fire the cycle of nature, and is itself set on fire by hell."[4] In 2018, a teenager was playing with fireworks, and accidentally started a two-month wildfire that burned more than 48,000 acres. The teen was charged $36 million in restitution.[5] The seemingly harmless act from a naive teenager caused a blaze that devastated businesses and homeowners throughout northern Oregon. In the same way, the small things that we say can have devastating effects in the lives of those around us.

Nicknames are like a firework in a dry gorge.

I understand why people give demeaning nicknames to others. The words of another person carry less power if we consider that other person to be 'lesser.' In houseless advocacy work, angry neighbors can say incredibly hurtful things. It is easier to disregard these attacks if we stereotype all neighbors as NIMBYs. However, to stereotype neighbors as NIMBYs is to remove a little bit of their humanity, and that makes me uncomfortable.

---

[4] James 3:5-6

[5] "Teen who started massive Oregon wildfire with fireworks must pay $36 million, judge rules," Washington Post, May 22, 2018, https://www.washingtonpost.com/news/post-nation/wp/2018/05/21/teen-who-started-massive-oregon-wildfire-with-fireworks-must-pay-36-million-judge-rules/

I received an email from a lady who lives close to the site of the proposed Village. She wanted to speak with me about our plans, and to voice her concerns and frustrations. I went to her house and listened to her talk about the money that she was saving to move into a retirement home. The sale of her house was going to be a major reason why this move would be financially possible. She was worried that, were we to implement this Village, her property would lose enough value as to make her retirement plans impossible.

Another group of neighbors talked to me about their children who attend the adjacent elementary school. They were concerned that if a sheltering program were to exist so close to the school, it would attract more houseless people to the area. This, in turn, could invite more drug use, violence, and crime to the neighborhood, and could threaten the safety of the children at the school. Moreover, there was a fear that if too many people were to pull their students out of this school because of the nearby Village, then the school would have to close its doors. One of these neighbors said to me, "I think what we all want is the same thing--we all want our children to be safe."

Although I disagree with these neighbors (our plans for the program and security are solid, and the entrance to the Village is nowhere near the school. Moreover, there is no concrete evidence linking Village programs to a decrease in neighborhood housing prices[6])

---

[6] "No Link Between Homeless Villages and Crime Rates, Guardian Review Suggests," The Guardian, May 23, 2018, https://www.theguardian.com/us-news/2018/may/23/homeless-villages-crime-rate-seattle-portland

their fears are completely understandable. Fears about the future and about safety are valid and relatable, and I do not want to brush aside these fears simply because these folks disapprove of our project.

Those that consider this to be the wrong place are, yes, predominantly neighbors and community members. However, they are multidimensional people with real concerns about their future and their families. While we disagree, and while I often become aggravated by their comments, attacks, and occasional slander, I also feel this deep compassion for their fears. When the status quo has worked for you, upsetting the status quo is scary.

On the flip side, when the status quo has not worked for an entire group of people, it often needs to be upset.

There is another tiny home Village about three miles away from our church. This Village is located a few blocks from another neighborhood, but not immediately in the middle of it. It has existed for a few years and has been quite successful in providing safety and security, as well as in moving many of its residents into permanent housing. This Village has been one of the models that our team has pointed toward as an example of how a Village can be successful.

Early on in my conversations with neighbors, I became deflated when I realized that this nearby Village was not seen as a good comparison to what we were promoting. The reasoning for this was that our Village was within a residential area, and that Village was in an industrial area. Many neighbors argued that our Village could work, were it located in an industrial area that would not attract crime or violence.

I have a couple of fundamental problems with this sentiment. First, the argument that 'the Village should be located in an industrial area' is an argument that the houseless folks who will reside in the Village do not deserve the same dignity as those who are able to live in a residential area; who are able to pay $450,000 for a house. Part of what attracted me to the model of a tiny home Village was the understanding that these homes would exist within a community, and would be built by developers and designed to fit the aesthetic of the community. The Village would offer the dignity of a local home, with the safety and security needed by the most vulnerable in society. The argument that 'the Village should be located in an industrial area' implicitly makes the claim that the residents of the Village are not deserving of the same respect and dignity that is granted to the middle and upper class of society.[7]

In my view, the appeal of a Village located within a residential area is the dignity that would be offered to people who rarely experience dignity. When I

---

[7] The sentiment that lower income individuals are less valued than mid-to-high income persons is one that was recently echoed by Donald Trump while he was President: "Trump Tweets About Suburban Lifestyle Dream," ABC 7 Chicago, July 29, 2020, https://abc7chicago.com/trump-tweet-suburban-lifestyle-dream-suburb/6340805/

consider the question "Where would be the right place," I think we need to consider what kind of future that we want for our city and for this world.

I want a more equitable society than we have right now.

I want a city where there is a smaller gap between rich and poor.

I want a society that has more people considering themselves worthy of dignity and respect, because they have been offered dignity and respect by their neighbors.

I want to show our children that it is possible for people to move from social outcast to valued community citizen.

I want to show the world that this kind of redemption is possible.

Dignity is powerful. Dignity gives hope. Dignity helps a person imagine themselves in a future that's better than the one in which they currently exist. I have experienced dignity in recent years. You probably have as well. To offer housing in a residential area, instead of banishing our most vulnerable to a lesser venue, is an act of kindness; an act of compassion; an act of dignity.

Where is the right place?

I think the right place is right here.

For years, the churches of north Portland have come together to run an emergency warming shelter for the houseless. This shelter would operate every night that the temperature dropped below freezing. It was a massive undertaking. It is difficult to pull together trained volunteers to stay with the sheltering adults for the night. In addition, setup, teardown, and cleaning required a lot of hands.

In 2017, Portland experienced what was referred to as a "Snowpocalypse" (I grew up in southern Oregon, and would not consider the snow and ice that we experienced to be remotely "apocalyptic," but whatever). Hundreds of cars were abandoned on the freeways and highways, many businesses were closed for a couple of weeks, and most citizens had little idea of how to cope.

This also meant that the warming shelter was open *a lot* during that winter. A pastor from the church that was the site of the warming shelter called me one day to ask if our church would be willing to act as the shelter site for a few days. Their church had housed homeless people for so long that their church needed a top-down deep clean. It was smelly and disgusting.

We, of course, were happy to oblige. For three days the warming shelter met at our church. In those three days, there were only two issues. There was one small coffee stain on a couch, and there was a conflict that was quickly deescalated by one of the incredible volunteers. The whole thing went shockingly well, considering there were 50-60 people sleeping in a room together.

In those three days, the church received a decent amount of phone calls. Occasionally a houseless person went outside to smoke, or sat outside with their cat on their lap, and a neighbor or community member would call to complain. These complaints were mostly settled quickly. However, I cannot help thinking about the "if you see something, say something" attitude that we tend to have when it comes to houseless people. If I sat down on a curb to rest, nobody would think anything of it. However, a houseless person sitting on a curb with their cat causes us to immediately call an authority figure. We have a heightened sense - a stronger radar - when we notice houseless people.

I say "we," because I certainly have the same tendencies. Whenever I see a houseless person on our property at the church, my instinct is to make them leave immediately. I said earlier that I hate asking people to leave the church property, and I do. But I also admit that I do have an inherent prejudice about houseless people. I admit that I am often disgusted when I see a person panhandling. I have grown a lot as a person over the years, and these days my compassion very often outweighs my disgust. However, the disgust still exists. I often see a houseless person and have my defenses up. I am fully aware that houseless people are not, by nature, violent. However, my prejudice does sometimes cause me to worry about my own safety when I am around a houseless person. I understand why we received calls when the emergency warming shelter operated out of our church. I often have the same tendencies as many of our neighbors. I instinctively fear people who are different from me.

It makes me think about the question I posed earlier: "If *this* is the wrong place for a tiny home Village, then what kind of service to the homeless would be right in this place?" Whether it's a soup kitchen, an emergency shelter, or a tiny home Village, service to the homeless in our vicinity often fills us with fear. Inviting houseless people to our neighborhood is an act of courage, because our base instinct is to fear.

Many of the neighbors who argued, "I'm not anti-homeless; I just think this is the wrong place," said that a better solution would be for us to house people inside of our church building. I have two responses to that. First, tiny home Village projects became more widespread a few years ago because advocates talked with houseless people and asked what they desired. Villages were desired by many over single-building sheltering. Plus, there are other apartment-complex type buildings for housing in the Portland area. We are offering an alternative.

Second, I imagine that housing people in our building would invite the same complaints. In just three days, we received multiple calls about those who were coming to the warming shelter. That shelter *operated inside of our church building*. This leads me to believe that a different type of housing would not change people's thoughts. I do not think that a different type of houseless ministry would ease hearts and minds. I think the problem is our own fear, discrimination, and prejudice.

Would cancelling all ministries and outreach to the homeless ease our own fear and burdens.

Yes.

Yes it would.

But it would also leave our most vulnerable with the weight of the world on their shoulders.

I think the flourishing of houseless people throughout Portland is worth the fear and discomfort that we feel when faced with people different from us.

No, I do not think that this is the wrong place.

The dignity and flourishing of the disadvantaged and marginalized is worth our discomfort.

PART III: REFLECTING

I spent about a month stalking people online.

I wish that sentence wasn't true. I wish it was just an attention-getting sentence that I put at the top of this section to intrigue you enough to keep reading. I wish that you would find out in a few pages that I didn't *actually* stalk people, or that "stalk" was an exaggeration.

For months, our church leaders received angry letters from folks who were opposed to the Village. A hefty church of these were rage-fueled screeds telling us about how terrible we were for bringing something so awful into the community.

About a month into the publicizing of our project, we heard whispers that a lawyer was planning to sue our church, and that neighbors were paying all of the legal fees to make it happen. Sure enough, a couple months later we received a legal threat from said lawyer. Shortly after, we received a threat from another lawyer representing a real estate person who owned properties in the area. We sought legal counsel and responded to them as needed. Near the end of the year, our church began receiving letters from community members who threatened to sue the church. Over a hundred of these came to the church within about a month. Our Neighborhood Association sent us a letter telling us that they would support, back, and endorse any neighbors who were willing to follow through in a lawsuit.

Obviously these letters were upsetting, but we were not terribly concerned about the future of the project. We had legal counsel, and all parties associated with the project were careful to dot all i's and cross all t's. We were careful not to leave ourselves open to litigation.

Time passed, and 2019 turned to 2020. We signed a lease, and the project began moving forward in earnest. A petition was started online to shut down our project. The comments section of this petition became heated.

I broke Rule 1 of the internet: Never Read the Comments Section.

I read them all. I obsessed. I am not sure if I was tired of being attacked and slandered for almost a year, or if my curiosity was getting the best of me. All I know is that hardly an hour went by without my checking if someone new had said something negative about me or about our church. I watched for specific names. I memorized faces. I didn't have a plan for retaliation. I just wanted to know who my enemies were.

I held on to every angry letter; every lawsuit threat. I read them over and over. I still had the original threat from the neighborhood lawyer; a threat that was cosigned by many of our neighbors, with names and addresses attached. I began cross-checking addresses with names and pictures from Facebook threads and the petition's comments section. I looked up addresses on Google Maps so I would know where many of these folks lived. I scrolled through Facebook, Instagram, and Twitter feeds, looking for any kind of negative information. I was not planning to do anything with this information; I just wanted it in my head.

I wanted to Know My Enemy.

Ash Wednesday 2020 soon approached, and I began to plan our Ash Wednesday service. Ash Wednesday is a day where the church across the world practices *repentance*: a fancy church word that simply means "turning from sin and back to God." Oftentimes Christians will repent of their individual sins (greed, envy, lust, racism, anger, hatred), or for ways in which the church as a whole has been sinful (the pursuit of power or money over God, discrimination of all kinds, spiritual abuse). I was in prayer, asking God to convict me of the ways in which I had been sinful. Quickly I was confronted with the reality that I had been wholly unable to forgive those who had hurt me over the past year. My obsession with faces, names, addresses, and the language people used about my church and I were rooted in my unforgiveness toward those who hurt me.

The fact is, whether or not my neighbors were correct in their opinions about our project, I had begun to see them as nothing more than enemies. I had reduced their humanity to their opinions about my church. My neighbors were no longer neighbors; they were enemies. I had dehumanized them in my mind. Scrolling obsessively through their social media pages was my attempt to find problematic things written by or about them, so that I could feel superior.

It was wrong.
It was sinful.
I needed to repent.

I justified the online stalking of my neighbors by telling myself that I was never going to hurt them in any way. I would never vandalize their homes. I would not even go to their homes uninvited to talk to them. However, my intentions were to know as much as I could about them, so that I could feel superior to them.

I needed to repent.

More than that, I needed to learn to forgive.

The writer of Luke and Acts (same dude, both books) weaves a theme of forgiveness throughout both books. In Jesus' Sermon on the Plain in Luke 6, he says,

> But I say to you that listen, Love your enemies, do good to those who hate you, bless those who curse you, pray for those who abuse you. If anyone strikes you on the cheek, offer the other also; and from anyone who takes away your coat do not withhold even your shirt. Give to everyone who begs from you; and if anyone takes away your goods, do not ask for them again. Do to others as you would have them do to you. If you love those who love you, what credit is that to you? For even sinners love those who love them. If you do good to those who do good to you, what credit is that to you? For even sinners do the same. If you lend to those from whom you hope to receive, what credit is that to you? Even sinners lend to sinners, to receive as much again. But love your enemies, do good, and lend, expecting nothing in return. Your reward will be great, and you will be children of the Most High; for he is kind to the ungrateful and the wicked. Be merciful, just as your Father is merciful.[8]

In theory, forgiveness seems great. In practice, however, it can often be seemingly impossible. How can those who lost everything forgive Bernie Madoff? How can victims of abuse forgive their abusers? How can my

---

[8] Luke 6:27-36

LGBTQ friends (and their loving family members) forgive those who have disowned them or called them abominations? Honestly, were I in any of these positions, I don't know if I could forgive.

Forgiveness is hard.

Really hard.

The writer does not spend the rest of Luke and Acts passionately arguing that people should forgive. Honestly, it would probably fall on deaf ears. Jesus said it once, and he said it clearly. Rather, Luke shows Jesus and other early Christians *modeling* forgiveness.

On the cross, Jesus looked down at those who spat at him, who beat him, who mocked him, who forced him to carry a cross, who nailed him to that cross, and who waited for him to die, and he said "Father, forgive them; for they do not know what they are doing."[9] Jesus modeled forgiveness for his people, and it wouldn't have been easy. After all, he did it while bleeding to death on a cross.

Similarly in the book of Acts, Luke writes about a man named Stephen, who was to be stoned. He was asked if he had any last words, and after giving a ridiculously long speech, they began to stone him. As he was dying, Stephen cried out, "Lord, do not hold this sin against them."[10] The writer knew that forgiveness is difficult, so he again showed it in action.

---

[9] Luke 23:34
[10] Acts 7:60

The unfortunate truth is that people in life will hurt us. Sometimes they hurt us so deeply that it feels like murder. Another unfortunate truth is that many times, those people who hurt us believe that they are acting honorably. Jesus and Stephen's killers *thought they were doing God's will* by killing them. Some friends of mine who have been disowned by their families have been deeply, and possibly irreparably, damaged by these family members. However, those family members believed that they were simply speaking truth honorably, and in so doing, they wounded one of God's children.

Well-meaning people will hurt you.

Well-meaning people may try to destroy you.

Well-meaning people saw in Stephen someone who perverted God's word. On the other hand, Stephen saw in them people of faith who, while wildly misguided and wrong, missed the amazing thing God was doing in the world through Jesus. He saw people who had a chance. He saw people who might find hope in this world yet.

Unforgiveness seeks to harm, while forgiveness seeks to heal.

Unforgiveness sees only evil in another person, while forgiveness sees potential.

The early church had to learn this truth. Paul, one of the people responsible for the death of Stephen and many other early Christians, became an ardent follower of Jesus. But after his conversion, the early Christians feared him (for obvious reasons) and doubted his role as a disciple. This is one of the most interesting situations in all of scripture. One of the greatest evangelists and missionaries to ever live was one of the enemies of the Gospel. Can you imagine if the Christian community never forgave Paul? It would not be unthinkable. Honestly, they didn't need to accept him as one of their own. In fact, it seems downright reasonable *not* to forgive him. He was an enemy of Jesus' followers. He was instrumental in the death of many of the early Christians; friends of theirs. Were I in their shoes, I probably would have sent Paul packing.

But they forgive Paul.

They practice forgiveness, because that is what Jesus taught them.

It's what Jesus modeled for them.

In the Sermon on the Mount, Jesus says "You have heard it said, love your neighbor and hate your enemy. But I say to you, love your enemies and pray for those who persecute you."[11] Loving enemies is hard work. It is especially hard work after months, or even years of feeling slighted or attacked by them.

---

[11] Mt. 5:33-34

I realized that my neighbors--my literal neighbors--had become my enemies over the course of the year.

My unforgiveness had kept me from learning to love them.

My unforgiveness had caused me to stalk them instead.

I needed to practice what Jesus taught,
what Jesus modeled,
what Stephen modeled,
what the early church practiced.

I needed to forgive those who wronged me.

We often have to ask people to stop camping on the church property.

It sucks.

It's terrible.

In Matthew 5, Jesus begins his longest sermon by saying,

> "Blessed are the poor in spirit, for theirs is the kingdom of heaven.
> Blessed are those who mourn, for they will be comforted.
> Blessed are the meek, for they will inherit the earth.
> Blessed are those who hunger and thirst for righteousness, for they will be filled.
> Blessed are the merciful, for they will receive mercy.
> Blessed are the pure in heart, for they will see God.
> Blessed are the peacemakers, for they will be called children of God.
> Blessed are those who are persecuted for righteousness' sake, for theirs is the kingdom of heaven."[12]

And in his first public message from the book of Luke, Jesus reads these words from the prophet Isaiah:

---

[12] Mt. 5:3-10

"The Spirit of the Lord is upon me, because he has anointed me to bring good news to the poor. He has sent me to proclaim release to the captives and recovery of sight to the blind, to let the oppressed go free, to proclaim the year of the Lord's favor."[13]

These passages swirl in my mind whenever I need to ask houseless people to leave our property. It feels completely anti-Christ to send people away from the church when their only crime is trying to rest their head and find refuge from the rain. Jesus' blessings and freedoms proclaimed in these texts are for the poor, the blind, the mourning, the meek, and the prisoners. The church should be a refuge for these folks. How can a person--especially a pastor--force someone to leave the shelter of the church? The truth is, I probably shouldn't. But I have. Many times. A pastor friend of mine says that asking people to stop sleeping on the church property "feels like crucifying Christ all over again."

It is easy to justify having to make houseless people leave the church property. After all, whenever one person sleeps on the property, inevitably more people show up. There is a practicality to stopping our church property from turning into a full-blown homeless camp. I can justify my choices by telling myself that if we were to allow a bunch of people to sleep on our property, we would certainly cause problems with the neighbors around the church. All of these things are true.

---

[13] Lk. 4:18-19

However, I cannot make a biblical case for turning people away from our church building, if their only crime is needing a place to sleep.

Jen Butler, a pastor in Corvallis and a hero of mine, was interviewed about a homeless camp that her church was supporting near their church building. When asked why her church would involve themselves in this kind of work, she responded "When Jesus shows up on your front door, you take care of Jesus."[14]

Often when Jesus shows up on our doorstep, I don't take care of Jesus.

I send Jesus away.

Two tents showed up on our church property one Monday morning in May of 2019. I, somewhat annoyed, went outside to tell the people in the tents to leave the property. One of the people said okay, but the other one stammered a little bit, and then said, "We were told that we could be here."
"No, that's not true," I replied. "This is private property, and you can't camp here. I'm sorry."
"Well, we were told that our friend spoke with you, and that you gave us permission to stay here."
I asked about this friend, and it was someone I knew; a local homeless advocate. I reiterated that they could not

---

[14] "You Take Care of Jesus," KGW News, accessed Jan. 28, 2021, https://www.kgw.com/article/news/local/homeless/corvallis-church-help-homeless-despite-legal-confusion-angry-neighbors/283-132db0af-e7bb-441e-a7e7-9387ce979be5

stay on the property long-term, and I went back inside the church. Once inside, I reached out to this advocate. She and I had a short text exchange. I asked if she gave permission for these folks to camp on the property, which she denied. It was quick; it was painless. I went to my office and worked for a few hours.

Later that day, I went back outside. Two tents had now become five. I walked back to the group and told them, once again, that they couldn't camp on the premises. All of them once again pointed me back to the same advocate. I wrote her back, a little more pointedly. "More people are on the property, and we simply cannot have them camping on the property." After once again denying sending the group to the church lot, she went for the jugular.

Are you really going to send them away? They have nowhere to go. You are a church.

This text has haunted me for over a year. Again, I had plenty of reasons to justify sending the campers away:

"We're not insured for people to live on the premises. If someone is hurt on our property, we could be responsible."
"The neighborhood is never going to allow a camp like this to remain here."
"If we allow people to stay, more are going to show up."
"We've already upset the neighborhood with the announcement of the Village. We don't want to antagonize people even more."

All of these points were true. However, this advocate was also 100% correct.

We are a church.

We are a church who asked poor people in need to pack up their stuff and leave.

We are a church who turned away the hungry and the needy.

I am a pastor who turned away the oppressed, the downtrodden, and the homeless.

I was haunted by this reality then. I am haunted by it now.

I looped in the folks from the county and from Do Good Multnomah. Both groups agreed that while it would be lovely to allow people to sleep on our land, our relationship to the neighborhood was tenuous enough that we needed to refrain from antagonizing them further.

More people showed up to the camp. More phone calls were made. More texts and emails were exchanged. I received an email from a friend who was involved in the discussions. He said "Stop messaging anyone associated with the camp immediately. Your texts and messages are being leaked to the local news."

Cool.

The police captain and the mayor's office were brought in on the discussion. The group emails and texts were rocketing back and forth, as we discussed how to-- firmly but compassionately--remove the campers from the property.

Willamette Week and KGW News started messaging and calling me for an interview. A communications representative from the county messaged me, saying that it would be helpful if I did an on-camera interview.

Please understand my state of mind at this point. I was trying to come to grips with the fact that I was on phone call after phone call, figuring out how to kick 20+ people off of our property. I was doing my best to ignore the cries of the downtrodden, oppressed, and hurting; to focus solely on keeping our Village project alive. And now I was preparing to go on camera to tell the entire city of Portland that our church would not tolerate the presence of suffering people.

It sucked.

An hour after being asked to do an interview, a KGW News camera faced me, and the interviewer spoke the words, "So this is what the neighborhood feared, isn't it?" I spent the next five minutes passionately arguing that our church did not endorse this camp, that the people needed to leave immediately, and that our Village would be considerably more appealing than the one that currently existed on the site.

I felt gross saying it. I feel gross right now as I'm writing about it.

After the interview went live, a local advocate made a call for other activists and supporters to show up at the church to fight on behalf of the camp. When I came to work the next morning, I had a slew of impassioned messages from activists across the city. I also had quite a few messages from neighbors, demanding that I remove the camp immediately.

By Friday, the police captain and a crew of officers (on my order) came to the church to deliver a trespass order to each of the campers. It felt awful. I was accused of laughing and hi-fiving my friends when the campers were told to leave (I don't know what this person thought they saw, but it definitely was not that). I felt terrible for making the people leave the church property. I felt angry and misunderstood when we were referred to online as "Pastor David and his flock of a-- holes." I was irritated when our church's Facebook page was hit with 1-star reviews for kicking out the homeless.

I learned a couple of important things on this particular week. First, people are going to believe whatever they want about you, and there is little to nothing that you can do about it. The neighborhood hated me. Homeless advocates hated me. This little project that our church was doing to try and help people made me an enemy to many. That's a burden I had to carry for a time.

Second, we live in tension. Doing good for one group often seems to require that we ignore another group, at least for a time. I knew that the future of our

Village project was potentially threatened by the existence of the camp on our property. We were already facing a couple of possible lawsuits, and we could not afford to antagonize some of our neighbors (especially our wealthy neighbors) further. Plus, we did not have the insurance capabilities to properly house this camp. It seemed impossible to allow them to stay.

On the other hand, the advocates and activists were absolutely correct:

Jesus came to bring good news to the poor, and we failed to bring good news to these campers.

We gave them bad news; terrible news.

I constantly wonder what would have happened, had I gone to the mat defending this camp. I wonder what the future of the Village project would have been like, had I told the neighborhood that we would allow the camp to remain on our property.

It may have caused more issues and headaches for us, but it would have felt a lot more Jesusy.

At our first informational community meeting, an older gentleman came to the front of the Q & A line. He began his speech like many others, talking about how he'd lived in St. Johns for many years, and in his time here he had seen a lot of changes to the community. He ranted about the large influx of houseless folks over the past decade, and how much of a problem he felt it had become.

After his intro, he said, "These people expect us to pay for their food, their medical care, and their clothes. Our taxpayer dollars pay for their drugs." And then he took the air out of the room with this line:

I don't even call them people. I call them parasites.

This rhetoric is demeaning and hateful. Referring to people without homes as "parasites" is abhorrent. Full stop. Thankfully, the crowd agreed, and they shouted him down.

Dehumanizing groups of people causes us to feel even more negativity and disgust toward them. As Brené Brown writes, "During the Holocaust, Nazis described Jews as Untermenschen—subhuman. They called Jews rats and depicted them as disease-carrying rodents in everything from military pamphlets to children's books. Hutus involved in the Rwanda genocide called Tutsis cockroaches. Indigenous people are often referred to as savages. Serbs called Bosnians aliens. Slave owners throughout history considered slaves subhuman animals."[15] A former professor of mine, Ed McIndoo,

---

[15] Dehumanizing Always Starts with Language," Brené Brown, May 17, 2018,

once said that the two most important questions that we can ask a person, both as a ministry leader and as a friend, are "What is your name?" and "What is your story?" He pointed out that during the Holocaust, imprisoned Jews were given numbers instead of names in order to make it easier to torture them. If we are quick to learn a person's name and story, we are considerably less likely to demean or dehumanize them in the future. If we look at a houseless person--a beloved child of God--as nothing more than a parasite, then it is easier for us to hate and demean that person.

So, no. I do not endorse this gentleman's description of Portland's houseless population as "parasites."

They are people--people who are loved by God.

However, as the months have passed since this encounter, I have asked myself repeatedly whether I implicitly dehumanize our houseless neighbors, without using the same kind of language. Do I consider houseless folks to be "parasites," whether or not I say the term out loud?

As I write this, there are many people camping on the street in front of and around our church building. Others are camping on the sidewalk. They have been there for months. I have often noticed myself becoming increasingly frustrated with the campers. On more than one occasion, I considered calling the cops and having them immediately sent away from our property. This is

---

https://brenebrown.com/blog/2018/05/17/dehumanizing-always-starts-with-language/

not because they are causing a problem; quite the opposite actually. They are keeping their belongings together and as close to the curb as possible. They are kind and considerate, and try hard to be good neighbors. Yet I am still frustrated by their presence. I simply want them gone.

I have been trying to figure out why I seem to have more NIMBY in me than I previously thought. Ultimately, I think I still have quite a bit of trauma from That Meeting, where I absorbed the anger of hundreds of my neighbors, and I fear that a camp directly outside of our church will result in another three-hour screamfest. I do not want to relive that night. I often find myself wanting to send away houseless folks, simply because I know that their presence may result in other neighbors' anger toward me.

Over the past two years, I have been one of the faces of Portland faith leaders who care for houseless folks, but I also have frequent moments (or days, or even weeks) of frustration, where I want to shut the whole thing down.

It is easy to criticize others for their language.

It is much more difficult to examine the state of our own hearts.

Shortly after we announced the Village, someone made a comment in a Facebook group that shocked our entire pastoral team (to this day we still talk about it). In a comment thread dedicated to complaining about the project, this guy said, "Christian compassion is killing our community."

There's a lot to unpack here.

Compassion.... bad?
Killing our community?
What kind of community is this dude looking for? A violent, angry community? A compassionless community?

Honestly, I was flabbergasted when I first read that comment. Who could possibly be opposed to compassion? I know plenty of people who think that organized religion of any sort is detrimental to society. However, even these folks certainly understand that compassionate living is good for society, whether or not it comes from religious or spiritual people.

Someone responded to this guy, asking "What makes Christian compassion different from regular compassion?" The guy responded, "Christian compassion does not ask for anything in return." I've considered that statement for a couple of years, and the conclusion to which I keep returning is this:

Yep.

That's true. Christian compassion does not ask for anything in return. *Discipleship* requires everything of a Christian, but the compassion that a Christian expresses should not and does not require anything in return. However, coming to that conclusion asks a *ton* from me. If Christian compassion asks nothing in return, then my own practice of compassion will inevitably make me uncomfortable.

I recently asked a person living in his truck to leave our property for what seems like the 400th time. He's been there for a very, very long time. I have called the police on him. At times I have been kind to him, and at other times I have been a jerk. I have been everything in between. Every day I become more and more frustrated with this person, this truck, and the fact that they are still on our property.

This person has accused me of being a liar, called me an a--hole, and told me that I'm full of s---. He said that my Christianity is false, because I am not inviting the poor to "come unto me," and am instead banishing them. He told me that I should step down as a pastor because of how bad of a person of faith I am.

These comments weigh on me. They weigh on me so much. As the pastor of a church in the middle of a residential area, I feel this immense pressure to care for the homeowners in our neighborhood. I want to be a good neighbor as an individual, and on behalf of our church. Therefore, my inclination is to ask people to leave if they are causing problems or making large messes all over the property, sidewalk, or the street.

However, when people remind me of Jesus' words, whether in good faith or not, I feel a tremendous amount of guilt. I can never shake the thought that those arguments are right.

The Gospel *is* one-sided.

Jesus' love does not diminish if there is no reciprocity.

It is a one-sided love that continues giving and giving, whether or not any love comes back.

Christian compassion requires nothing in return.

My compassion toward others should be completely one sided. I should not offer compassion to others *only if* they become the way that I desire. That is the conundrum into which Christian compassion puts me. Do I continue allowing this guy to park at our property, even if he's being a nuisance? Do I continue to allow the camp on our sidewalk to remain, even though pedestrians now have to walk on the street because the entire sidewalk is blocked? Do I need to show compassion that asks nothing in return?

If I ask people to leave, am I showing "Christian compassion," or am I only showing compassion to those who show reciprocity?

Honestly, I do not know.

I don't even know if there is a correct answer.

I was not often faced with these kinds of questions before we announced the Village.

Now that our church (and I as its pastor) am being closely watched by some in our neighborhood, I have to wrestle through what it means to be compassionate as a pastor. I have to ask myself how my decisions reflect on the church that I lead; how they reflect on Christians everywhere. Anytime I instinctively call the police to have a houseless person moved, I have to question my motives. Am I modeling compassion to the community?

Having to ask myself these questions is hard. It is so hard. It certainly makes my job more difficult. However, I have come to believe that it is good and right and healthy to have to struggle through these questions. If my thoughts and instincts hinder the livelihoods of the vulnerable around me, then something is sincerely wrong with the condition of my heart. If my response to someone's proximity to me is to ask an armed authority to forcibly remove them, then my response is likely problematic.

If my desire as a Christian is to treat others the way that I want to be treated (and it should be), then I should be troubled by some of these instincts.

Housing the houseless put our church under a magnifying glass in the community, and that attention forced me to consider my thoughts and actions on a grander scale. It has been hard, but ultimately, I think it has been for my good. I think it has been for the good of our church. I think it's what God wants for us.

Throughout this process, some folks in opposition to the Village have said things like "This is a dying church, and they needed to find a way to pay the bills. That's the only reason they are doing this project." It is difficult to respond to this argument, because in some ways, they have a point. We could be considered a 'dying church.' We are a church that has significantly less people than it used to. In its heyday, our church had between 300 and 400 members attending regularly. When I arrived in 2015, there were around seventy. For a time, we grew to around a hundred people, but we quickly fell to between fifty and sixty.

Those in opposition to the Village were correct about our dire financial situation. After all, less people at the church means less money coming in, and less money coming in makes it hard to keep the church running. They are also correct in pointing out that our church is leasing our land to make this project a reality. We receive $3400 per month for the use of this land. I honestly understand the criticism levied against our church. I understand why people would not want us to receive money for this project.

I've had to ask myself painful questions, such as "Is my own desire for the church to stay open causing me to try and justify our lease, or is this simply a greedy and selfish act on my part?" The answer is...I don't know. Are we, as some of our neighbors say, moving forward on this project with dollar signs in our eyes? I hope not, but maybe?

At the very least, those who claim that I'm greedy--that I want nothing more than to make myself and our church wealthy--are not crazy for holding that belief.

I have a ton of anxiety and tension regarding the financial piece of this project. I think the difficulty that I have with our church receiving money for this project is simply that it *feels* wrong. Is it wrong? Honestly, I don't know. I will say that when this project was pitched to me in early 2019, the money was certainly a large part of the appeal. Our church had been in a season of prayer about the future. We had spent over a year praying about two specific things. We asked God to help us with our church's financial difficulties, and we asked God to show us clearly what God wanted for us as a church. The truth is, when we were introduced to this plan, it became clear that this would be an answer to both of our prayers.

This would have been a much more difficult project to pitch to the congregation if money was not a part of the deal. Truthfully, I do not think that I would have personally been as excited about the project had there been no money involved. Just writing these words makes me deeply uncomfortable. Honestly, it feels gross to admit that I wanted to receive money in exchange for helping houseless people.

Moreover, of our church leadership, I was actually the most aggressive about the financial piece of this project. When our leadership first discussed the terms of this project, the rest of our leadership lowballed the amount of money that they wanted our church to receive. I, on the other hand, was pitching amounts much higher than where we finally settled. I reasoned that if the county was offering to pay us to be a part of this project, we might as well take the money. After all, it would help our church financially in the long run, and would keep us from being strapped for cash the way that we had been for years.

I believe with all of my heart that our church provides a lot to the community. I believe that our presence is still important in north Portland. I believe strongly that it is important for our church to stick around. However, I also wonder whether or not the financial piece of this project was far too important to me, especially in the early days.

The Rich Young Ruler was told to give all of his money to the poor before following Jesus. I was willing to serve the poor, but my own church's cashflow was a consideration of mine throughout the process. Were I in the Rich Young Ruler's shoes, I don't know if I would have followed Jesus. I, too, would certainly have been sad.

I am constantly grateful for our church leaders: Mike, Janel, Loren, Bud, Derek, Karen, and Jan for their wisdom throughout this project. My priorities were not always in the right place, and they kept me focused on the right things.

I do not have a good answer to the question, "Was it right to receive money in exchange for this work?" The money was offered to us, and it absolutely helped our church financially. It has allowed us to continue moving forward as a church, and to continue doing ministry without the imminent fear of having to close our doors. However, as I said previously, it feels gross and kind of immoral.

I actually think that "Was it right to receive money in exchange for this work?" is the wrong question to ask. At the very least, it is not a completely fulfilling question. This question is one about our morality as a church, and assumes a simple "yes" or "no" response. I actually think there is a far more important question to be asked alongside this first question.

Jesus' words on money and finances found in the Sermon on the Mount carry a lot of weight and expectation; expectation that is now on our church. As he says in Matthew 6,

> "Do not store up for yourselves treasures on earth, where moth and rust consume and where thieves break in and steal; but store up for yourselves treasures in heaven, where neither moth nor rust consumes and where thieves do not break in and steal. For where your treasure is, there your heart will be also.
> The eye is the lamp of the body. So, if your eye is healthy, your whole body will be full of light; but if your eye is unhealthy, your whole body will be full of darkness. If then the light in you is darkness, how great is the darkness!

No one can serve two masters; for a slave will either hate the one and love the other, or be devoted to the one and despise the other. You cannot serve God and wealth."[16]

To 'store up treasures in heaven' is to put all of your energy into living for God. To live for God is to treasure what God treasures; to love what God loves; to do as God asks; to see as God sees. To do so is to have healthy eyes that look toward the Light. Living for God keeps our priorities straight. It puts God's kingdom first above all other kingdoms. It puts God's plan above all other plans. It puts God's desire for the world above any other desires for the world. It puts flourishing for all people above suffering, hurt, and pain for some.

According to Jesus, living for God is a treasure that will not be destroyed, stolen, or consumed.

It is the treasure that will continue to be cherished long into the future.

Jesus compares life for God to a life in pursuit of wealth. He says that a life in pursuit of money is not only contradictory to a life in pursuit of God; he says that these lives cannot coexist at all. If we live in pursuit of money, we will not live in pursuit of God. Paul calls the love of money "the root of all kinds of evil"[17] because it invites all kinds of temptations into our lives. Many of us have known someone who has acted in terrible,

---

[16] Mt. 6:19-24
[17] 1 Tim. 6:10

abhorrent ways in order to gain money. Maybe you've been one of those people. The pursuit of money can cause us to act in opposition to God's ways and God's will. Greed gets a hold of us and causes us to do awful things.

As I consider whether or not our church made a mistake by accepting money in exchange for leasing our land for the Village, I am faced with another question; a question that is connected to the first:

How are you going to use this money to further God's kingdom?

Again, I am deeply uncomfortable with the accusation that I pushed this project forward solely to raise money for our church, because it makes me question whether or not that accusation is true. It is not unthinkable that greed was underlying my motives for this project. After all, I am a staff member of our church, and my paycheck comes from the church. Is it unthinkable that I was trying to keep my job secure for a few more years? I hope my motives were pure, but I often wonder if I acted out of self-preservation, at least on some level.

It is extremely important that our church honestly and prayerfully considers how we operate from this point forward. It is imperative that we consider Jesus' words carefully. Jesus is calling us to put our treasures in heaven; to put our highest priority into living for God alone. We have some new money because of this project. Our church is more stable financially than it was a year ago. We now have two options. We could settle into our new reality, where we profit off of this project and become complacent as a church. Our staff would be financially secure, and our church could last for at least a few more years; perhaps a few more decades.

Conversely, we could use this money to further God's kingdom in north Portland. There are an enormous amount of needs in our community; from housing, to hunger, to harm reduction, to mental health issues, to clothing needs, to safety issues involving vulnerable kids and teenagers. We have an opportunity to meet needs on a level that we could not achieve before.

"Was it right to receive money in exchange for this work?" is an important question. Truly, it is essential that I consider my motives as I lead our church, and I am grateful to many of our neighbors for calling me out and forcing me to do so. However, it is equally imperative that our church consider the question "How are you going to use this money to further God's kingdom?" We must not consider the opening of the St. Johns Village to be the conclusion of our involvement in this project. Rather, we now have a responsibility to use our new money wisely and well. We have a responsibility to steward our money to bring God's mercy, grace, love, and justice to our city.

We have a responsibility to put our treasures in heaven; not in our earthly treasures.

My greatest desire for this book is that someone who is considering doing any kind of Jesusy work in the realm of housing or homelessness will see that it is possible to finish the work in spite of resistance and slander. The work is hard, and most of the time it feels thankless. You will be hated by neighbors, community members, housing advocates, and even the people that you are trying to help. It will frustrate you beyond belief, and every forty-seven seconds you will want to quit. I hope this book can be a reminder that the work is worth it, and that the vision can ultimately come to fruition.

I wish this book could function as a how-to manual for people who want to house houseless folks. However, I do not have a wealth of advice for anyone who is striving to replicate our efforts. Our church began this project with an idea, a conviction, and not one iota of know-how. I have been completely out of my element through this whole process. I do not have a background in housing, homelessness, city planning, nonprofit law, or zoning codes. We went into this project with no lawyer. We started this endeavor convinced that there would be a small resistance early on, but that it would quickly be dissolved once people heard our pitch (we were so young, adorable, and naive).

The point is, if you are looking for a detailed walkthrough of how your church can implement a housing solution in your community, you should look elsewhere. That being said, there have been some things that have helped our church (and I as their pastor) navigate this process over the last couple of years. Hopefully some of these will help you cope with the craziness that you will experience.

1. Have people around you who have your back

    If our church tried to do this work on our own, we would have quit after a week. Between zoning laws, government red tape, angry neighbors, lawsuit threats, and dozens of advocates (each of whom had a contradictory idea of what would be most helpful for our project), we would not have had a clue how to move forward. Thankfully, we began our project with two other teams of people who had a distinct vision and a plan for how to move forward. The Joint Office for Homeless Services had the funding and the background to be able to financially support the project, and Do Good Multnomah had the personnel and the resources to be able to manage the project. Both of them were ready to move forward in spite of resistance.

    Far more important than these two entities, however, were the pastors, community members, neighbors, friends, and colleagues around the country who supported our work throughout the process. Ministry leaders gathered together regularly during the year to pray for our church and our leadership. Friends and strangers sent postcards to our church, telling us about how proud they were of us and the work we were doing. Friends checked in to make sure I was mentally okay.

    There were moments during this endeavor where I thought that I wouldn't make it to the finish line. My therapist recommended that I have a small group of friends to call if I'm having low moments; especially when I had thoughts of suicide. I have called on some of these friends often, and they were always there for me. It was a huge relief for me during some very dark times. Now that I mention it, another great piece of advice is,

2. Get a therapist

Seriously. You'll want one. When the community outrage becomes too much, and you just want to scream "I CAN'T DO THIS ANYMORE PEOPLE ARE BEING SO RIDICULOUS AAAAAAHHHHH WHY DID I EVER DECIDE TO DO THIS I'M SO STUPID AND NOBODY LIKES ME AND I SHOULD GO LIVE IN A HOLE IN THE WOODS SOMEWHERE SO THAT NOBODY CAN FIND ME AND I WON'T HAVE TO DEAL WITH ANY OF THIS &@)$*@^& ANYMORE," your therapist will be there for you.

3. Recognize that nothing you do will make everybody happy

More accurately, recognize that *everything you do will make somebody unhappy*. It sucks. It's the worst. The most depressed that I became during this whole process were the times that houseless advocates blasted our church online because of the choices that we made. In the same week, one advocate called us, "Pastor David and his flock of a--holes," and another told me that "I must have forgotten the teachings of Jesus."
Decisions I've made have caused people to call me a liar, a cheat, selfish, greedy, and a piece of s---.
Honestly, those kinds of things are hard to absorb.

This work is messy, and every decision is going to upset someone--even the people who seem like they should be on your side.

4. Use your relationships and connections

I do not like to ask others for help. In this kind of work, however, there are unexpected situations that will require more than you are able to provide. For example, none of us at the church had ever been threatened with a lawsuit before. We did not know how to find a lawyer, nor did we have the money to hire one. But when I reached out to the Joint Office for Homeless Services about our predicament, one of the people there talked with some connections and mentioned our situation. We got a call a few weeks later from a giant law firm in Portland who offered to represent us *pro bono*. Other people have connections and know-how that you do not. Use them.

5. Forgive yourself

You're going to screw up. A lot. You are going to make a ton of mistakes while doing this kind of work. It is easy to look back at what you could have done better. It will accomplish nothing to beat yourself up over mistakes that you have made.

Constantly recognize that you are doing the best that you can, and that's enough.

6. Grow a thick skin

Yeah, I'm terrible at this. It is easy to tell someone that they should grow a thick skin, but it is extraordinarily difficult for many of us to put it into practice. The fact is, though, that people are going to be angry with you. When you begin a project that involves homelessness, people will begin watching your church with an eagle eye and criticizing you for anything that they believe you have done wrong. You will be blamed for things beyond your control. Folks will suddenly notice the houseless people who have been in your community for months or even years, and will blame you for "bringing them here."

You are going to have to respond with grace, love, and mercy. You will need to accept that there are people in your community who hate you. You will hear some slander and accusations about yourself that are completely untrue, and that hurt deeply. There's nothing you can do about it.

Thankfully, it gets easier the more often that you do it.

7. You're going to be disappointed throughout

There were plenty of disappointments during this process. However, I assumed that once the tiny homes were built, the disappointments would mostly stop. That proved untrue.

The day that the tiny homes were lowered by crane into the Village location was one of the best days of my life thus far. As one of my co-laborers in this project said, "This feels like victory."

It really, truly did.

After two years of fighting with folks in the neighborhood, losing a few treasured relationships, being publicly slandered, and spending many nights wishing I was no longer among the living, I watched as all of our work was validated. Most of our crew showed up to witness the spectacle. Various news crews documented the occasion. It was truly a lovely day.

And then, two nights later, most of the homes were vandalized. Broken windows and doors; Glass littering the ground. A volunteer painting crew quickly became a cleanup crew. Even when the project was near its end, we had to deal with disappointment.

I also continue to be disappointed by the fact that a tiny-home Village for houseless folks is a deal-breaker for some of our neighbors. A surprising number of people have moved out of our neighborhood, citing the Village as their primary reason for leaving. On a practical level, it was helpful to the success of the project because they left. Were they to stay in the area, they would perpetually complain. However, it hurts my soul to think that the existence of houseless people in the neighborhood could cause someone to sell their home and move away.

8. Enjoy it

For a month or two, I felt like the most hated person in north Portland. The neighborhood was furious with our church for bringing "riffraff and vagrants" into the community. On the positive side, though, we were getting a ton of attention from local media. I was on the news within three days of our announcement, and quite a few times after. Our church appeared in local and statewide papers.

Honestly, that stuff was a ton of fun.

Our church has been slowly dwindling in attendance since the mid-90's, and it is often easy to miss the work that God is doing through our little community. But this work--people noticed it. It's rare to be noticed on a large scale for the work that you are doing. People all across the world have sent our staff messages, telling us how proud they are of us.

This is work that is often thankless. However, there are some elements that are fun. Enjoy them.

9. Don't stop

Don't stop. The work that you are doing is good. It is needed. It is indispensable.

In a world that contains both billionaires and the penniless, God's justice is needed.

Your work is needed.

Don't stop.

For the sake of the world, don't stop.

For the sake of the houseless among you, don't stop.

For the hard hearts in your community that need softening, don't stop.

For the people among you who need to see that houseless people are not all "drug-addled parasites," don't stop.

For the people in your church and in your city who need to see that this type of work is possible, don't stop.

For the sake of the other churches and community leaders who are quietly watching you to see if this work can be a success, don't stop.

You can make it to the finish line. You might be bleeding and bruised, but the work can be completed. It may take years, but it can be done.

It may bleed your church financially, but you can do it.

I was in a therapy appointment a few months into our project when I came to a realization: If we fail, God can still use it for good. Were our project to fail, the whole community would see it. The whole city would notice that our community shut down a little church who was trying to help the houseless, and likely that failure would spur others on to action.
Strangely, that idea kept me going.
Whether or not we were successful, God was going to use it. Therefore, we should keep going.

I'm glad we did.

I hope you keep going as well.

Our church has spent the last couple of years becoming deeply uncomfortable with the words of Jesus. When people think about Jesus, often they think of someone who was a good teacher, a peaceful leader, forgiving, loving, God in human flesh, or someone who died for the sins of the world. These things and more are all true of Jesus. However, it is equally true that any time spent reading the gospels will make a reader uncomfortable.

If you read the gospels (even one of them), Jesus will unsettle you. If you read the gospels and are not uneasy at something Jesus says, you didn't actually read the gospels. At the very least, you did not take them seriously.

Jesus makes us uncomfortable.

Our church has realized how uncomfortable Jesus' words and life can make us. After all, the things that Jesus said and did ended up putting him on a cross to die.

And he told us to take up our own crosses and follow him.

Jesus makes us uncomfortable. His teachings are radical and disturbing. As we grow and mature as Christians, we become progressively more in love with Jesus; often conversely, we become more uncomfortable with Jesus' call on our lives. We come to realize how much they require of us. Jesus knew this. He knew how radical and painful his teachings could be. He knew that when people follow him, they are going to encounter resistance.

In John 15, Jesus is speaking to his disciples, and addresses how they will encounter resistance because of his call on their lives. Jesus tells the disciples to abide in him and to love one another. He follows this by saying,

> "If the world hates you, be aware that it hated me before it hated you. If you belonged to the world, the world would love you as its own. Because you do not belong to the world, but I have chosen you out of the world—therefore the world hates you. Remember the word that I said to you, 'Servants are not greater than their master.' If they persecuted me, they will persecute you; if they kept my word, they will keep yours also. But they will do all these things to you on account of my name, because they do not know him who sent me."[18]

Abide in me and love one another.
Oh, and also, people are going to haaaaaaaate you.
They are going to freaking hate you.
They will persecute you.
They are doing it to me, and they are going to do it to you too.

Yikes.

---

[18] John 15:18-21

I have heard this passage of scripture preached and taught for my entire life. I grew up in a conservative evangelical context; specifically, one that had quite a large persecution complex. I was told throughout Sunday school, in youth groups, and in sermons, that I would be persecuted as a Christian. "One day," these church leaders sometimes said, "people might even want to kill you for being a Christian."[19] I think something deeper is happening in this text, however. Jesus' message and mission took him to the cross. The world hated Jesus because his message made people uncomfortable. He criticizes the Temple system in the book of Mark, and the text says immediately afterward, "They looked for a way to kill him."

Jesus' message wasn't popular with the powerful or the elites. It was not popular long-term with the masses. Jesus reversed what people expected, and he called people to costly living.

People don't like that.

Jesus knew that the disciples would experience a similar kind of thing. He knew that everybody who followed him afterward would experience a similar fate.

---

[19] I do not want to downplay any real, legitimate persecution that Christians or people of other religious backgrounds face worldwide today. There are real acts of persecution happening around the world that should trouble people of all backgrounds and beliefs. However, my teachers and church leaders were speaking to me as a young, white dude in a small-town church. These kinds of things were never going to happen to me, let's be real.

And beginning in 2019, our church started experiencing hate. We may not have experienced a gruesome and painful end like Jesus did, but we felt the sting of community hatred that comes from following Jesus' leading. After committing ourselves to this project, we had to live with the reality that people hated us and wanted to hurt us. That pressure was painful. It often made me want to quit--both the project, and at times even my role as pastor.

Our associate pastor, Derek, preached a message to our church early on in this process that has helped me remain grounded whenever the pressure became too much. He looked at a story from scripture in which God separates people into two groups, which he calls sheep and goats.[20] God looks toward one of the groups of people, the sheep, and says to them "Come, you that are blessed by my Father, inherit the kingdom prepared for you from the foundation of the world; for I was hungry and you gave me food, I was thirsty and you gave me something to drink, I was a stranger and you welcomed me, I was naked and you gave me clothing, I was sick and you took care of me, I was in prison and you visited me." The sheep are confused, as they don't remember doing any such thing. God responds by saying that whenever they did any of these things to someone else, especially the most vulnerable in society, they did it to God.

He then looks toward the goats and condemns them for the same thing. He says that they never fed the hungry, gave drink to the thirsty, welcomed the stranger,

---

[20] Matthew 25:31-46

clothed the naked, cared for the sick, or visited the prisoner.

It's a harsh story; again, one that should make us deeply uncomfortable. I know quite a few people in prison and can confess that I have not once visited any of them. Throughout this book, I have told stories of my failures to care for people around our church. These actions are hard and ask a lot from us. Feeding and bringing water to the needy takes time and effort. Offering shelter to those who don't have it can be dangerous. "Is this a safe person?" "How long are they going to stay?" "What if they don't leave?"
As we found throughout this project, even if you try to do it in the safest possible way, it's going to upset many people.

Jesus reminds us in this passage that we are accountable for the things that we did or failed to do. At the end of our lives, we have to live with the choices that we made, and if those choices led to the suffering of others, we are responsible for that.
Our church constantly tried to keep that in mind.
We tried.
And we sucked at it.
Boy, did we suck at it.
We made so many mistakes.
I made so many mistakes.
In the end, we're going to stand before Jesus with what we've done.

I have questioned my own motives often throughout the last couple of years, and here's where I keep landing:

We tried.

We tried hard.

And I am comfortable standing before Jesus with the work that we did. Our offering was filled with mistakes and disappointment. But ultimately, good was done.

We tried to do the right thing, and we did it because we believe it was the best thing for the world. We did it because we believe that God has a plan for us as a church, and for our city, and we wanted to join in the work that God was doing.

We had no idea what we were in for, but God used it for good.

It's difficult work that is at times soul-crushing.

But it was worth it.

It was so worth it.

Our tiny, scrappy, little rag-tag flock of sheep did our best, and I trust that God will use it for good.

ACKNOWLEDGEMENTS

I cannot overstate how much our church body accomplished in making the Village a reality. Strangely, most of our church members tell me that they feel they did little throughout this process. I have heard from a lot of folks that they are grateful to our church's leadership for the way that we have fought the good fight and taken the hits that we have. While it is true that our staff and leaders have taken the brunt of the public flak that came at us over the past couple of years, our church body was absolutely instrumental in making this project a reality.

Exodus 17 contains a couple of stories involving Moses' staff. In the second of these stories, the nation of Israel is at war with Amalek.[21] The battle was fought in a valley, but Moses stood on a hill with his staff in his hand. The story claims that whenever Moses' hand was raised in the air, the Israelites were victorious in battle. However, whenever Moses lowered the staff, the Israelites began losing the battle. Obviously, Moses' arm

---

[21] Stories like this one involving war, violence, and Israel as a nation are troubling through the lens of our modern world, and I find it irresponsible to use this story as a metaphor or connection point without acknowledging the difficulty of stories like this. Many of the violent actions of God's people in the early Old Testament are troubling and should not necessarily be seen as prescriptive for followers of God today. The world of the ancient Near East was a violent and tribal one, and violence over land was a common practice. God was speaking to a specific people in a specific time, and his commands to them would have been heard differently by people of that time. However, as we look at the arc of scripture, God moves his people from this sort of mentality to one where he commands people to "turn the other cheek," and to refrain from responding to violence with violence. We should not hear stories like this one and use them to rubber-stamp acts of violence in our world today.

became tired after holding his staff in the air for hours upon hours. However, the people of God relied on him to carry them through the battle. If he dropped his arm, all of God's people would be brutally slaughtered. So Aaron and Hur each braced Moses' arm in the air, so that the staff would remain raised and the Israelites would be victorious.

I often think of this story when I consider the trials associated with making the St. Johns Village a reality. The work of planning and implementing the Village was mostly done by the Joint Office for Homeless Services, Do Good Multnomah, and our building and architecture partners. Because our role was simply to lease our land, we did not provide much in the way of planning. The battle itself was predominantly fought by others. However, the entire project hinged on the involvement of our church. Without our land, the project as planned would not move forward. Do Good Multnomah and the Joint Office of Homeless Services needed our support, or they would not get to the finish line. For the past few years, I have felt like our leadership--myself, Janel, Derek, Loren, Karen, Bud, Jan, and Mike--have been Moses, standing on the hillside, making sure that the project was successful. However, being attacked by so many folks for so long made us tired.
Incredibly tired.
Exhausted.
Deflated.

At times, I wanted to lower the staff and go home.

Sure, the project would die. Sure, there would be
casualties.
But I was exhausted.
I was beaten.
I was bruised.
I wanted to quit.

However, over the course of the last two years, our
church body has braced me. They have supported our
leadership. They have convinced us to keep going. They
have supported us and kept our arm raised; our staff in
the air. The work was victorious, in part, because of the
support of our church.

If anything made this project a success, it was them.

Whenever someone paints our church body in a negative
light, it bothers me immensely, because I have seen
firsthand how loving, supportive, and committed to
God's work that they have been.

They made this happen.

I would not have been able to finish the work alone.
Our leadership could not have finished this work alone.
We needed to lean on the church, and I am so grateful
for their support, care, and kindness throughout the
whole process.

St. Johns Church: I love you. You did amazing work
over the past two years, and I can't wait to see what else
we can do over the next decade.

All of the leaders at our church have been incredible through this whole process: Janel, Derek, Loren, Karen, Bud, Jan, Mike, Matt, McKahan, and Josh—you all took a ton of hits, and I so appreciate it.

A ton of thanks go to my group of friends who help me get through each week intact, and who encouraged me to write all of this stuff down: Amy, Danielle, Jen, Jeannie, Connie, J.R., Jim, Marilyn, and Jessica.

To the whole crew who made this happen: Everyone at Do Good Multnomah, the Joint Office of Homeless Services, and Convergence Architecture. Specific thanks also to Andy, April, Denis, Jeremy, Marc, Chris, Joe, Lucas, Seraphie, Chris, Zachary, Kegan, Kanoelehua, Tara, Michelle, Nathan, Allen, and Adam – y'all are incredible.

Thank you to the hundreds of people who went to bat for us online and in person. All of you with St. Johns Welcomes the Village, every neighbor who called us or sent us a postcard, and everyone who had "spirited" conversations with neighbors and community members online and off - I'm so, so, so, so grateful to all of you.

I wrote most of this book on my phone while sitting in my car in random parking lots throughout Portland and Vancouver. Coffee shops weren't open during the pandemic, so the car was the only quiet place I had to write where I wouldn't be distracted.

I've heard that the 50 Shades of Grey author wrote that series on her phone as well, so I guess we have that in common. That's.....cool?

And a special thank you to my family: Liena, Lucy, and Zach. I've been a nightmare at home for much of the last two years because of the stress of this project, and you've been so great throughout.
I'm still so glad to be going through life with you.